This is one of a series of books on modern art created to help very young people learn the basic vocabulary used by artists, a sort of ABC of art. Parents and teachers play a key role in this learning process, encouraging careful, thoughtful looking. This book isolates shapes to show how they are used by artists and how they contribute to meaning in art. By looking at shapes and discussing what ideas and feelings they suggest, adults encourage children to develop creative thinking skills. At the back of this book, there is more information about the pictures included to help in this engaging process.

Enjoy looking together!

W9-BPK-216

Colors

Philip Yenawine

The Museum of Modern Art, New York
Delacorte Press

Acknowledgements
This book was made possible by the generosity of The Eugene and
Estelle Ferkauf Foundation; John and Margot Ernst; David Rockefeller,
Jr.; John and Jodie Eastman; Joan Ganz Cooney; and The Astrid
Johansen Memorial Gift Fund. Of equal importance were the talents of
Takaaki Matsumoto, Michael McGinn, Mikio Sakai, David Gale, Harriet
Bee, Richard Tooke, Mikki Carpenter, Nancy Miller, Alexander Gray,
Carlos Silveira, and particularly Catherine Grimshaw. I am extremely
grateful to all of them.

Library of Congress Cataloging in Publication Data

Yenawine, Philip.
Colors/by Philip Yenawine.
        p.   cm.
Summary: Isolates the artistic element of color, discusses what
thoughts and feelings can be conveyed by different colors, and exam-
ines how they contribute to a work of art through various examples.
ISBN 0-385-30254-1 (trade ed.). –ISBN 0-385-30314-9 (lib. ed.)
1. Color–Juvenile literature.   2. Color in art-Juvenile literature.
[1. Color.   2. Color in art.   3. Art appreciation.]   I. Title
QC495.5. Y46 1991
535.6–dc20   90–38984   CIP   AC

ISBN 0-87070-176-2 (MoMA)

The Museum of Modern Art
11 West 53 Street
New York, NY 10019

Delacorte Press
Bantam Doubleday Dell Publishing Group, Inc.
1540 Broadway
New York, New York 10036

Printed in Italy

May 1991

10   9   8   7   6   5   4   3   2

The world is full of colors.

Paul Signac, *Against the Enamel of a Background Rhythmic with Beats and Angles, Tones and Colors, Portrait of M Félix Fénéon in 1890*

That is a good thing, because colors are pretty and cheerful.

Claude Monet, *Water Lilies*

Detail of Monet, *Water Lilies*

But then again, colors can be serious and quiet.

Edward Steichen, *Moonrise, Mamaroneck, New York*

Sometimes colors can even seem a bit sad . . .

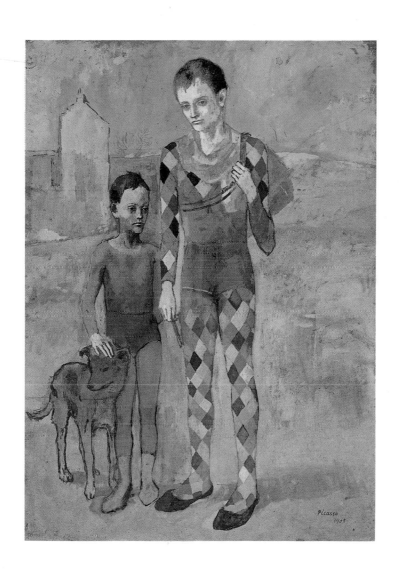

Pablo Picasso, *Two Acrobats with a Dog*

or mad!

Willem de Kooning, *Woman I*

Artists use colors to make designs.

Theo van Doesburg (C. E. M. Küpper), *Simultaneous Counter-Composition*

One artist may use many colors.

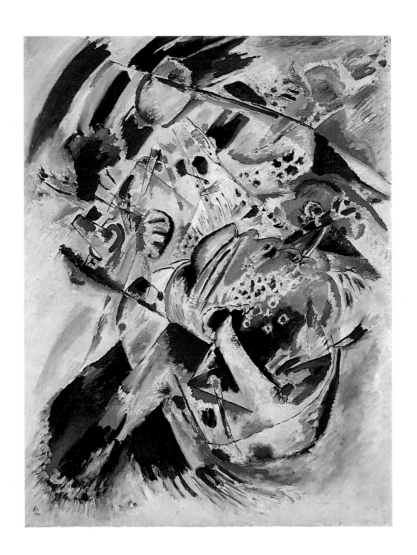

Vasily Kandinsky, *Painting Number 201*

Another may use shades of just one.

Josef Albers, *Homage to the Square: Broad Call*

Colors can be painted very neatly.

Frank Stella, *Abra Variation I*

Or messily. Does it make a difference?

Frank Stella, *Kastūra*

Colors can make things look very real . . .
and delicious.

Irving Penn, *Still Life with Watermelon*

**Sometimes they make things seem strange.
A pink street? Green and orange faces?
It's like a dream.**

Ernst Ludwig Kirchner, *Street, Dresden*

Colors can make a mountain village glow in the late afternoon sunlight.

Vasily Kandinsky, *Murnau Landscape*

Surrounded by purple and gold, summer flowers seem even more beautiful.

Odilon Redon, *Vase of Flowers*

Brighter than the moon, this light bulb seems to shoot out sparks of many-colored light.

Giacomo Balla, *Street Light*

Colors can command attention! Can you see that the light colors seem to come toward you? And the dark ones seem to sink in?

Hans Hofmann, *Cathedral*

Artists can make color puzzles. These bars of color show how you can mix two colors to get another.

Can you find all the colors you see in the color bars?

Jasper Johns, *Between the Clock and the Bed*

Look closely at this picture to see little dots of color. See how they blend together when you move back?

Georges-Pierre Seurat, *Port-en-Bessin, Entrance to the Harbor*

Here's a game. Can you imagine colors in place of the words?

Jasper Johns, *Jubilee*

Now that you have started imagining, maybe it's time to make some colorful pictures of your own—designs or stories, real or imaginary things. Can you use colors to make a noisy picture? A funny one?

The art in this book can be found at The Museum of Modern Art in New York City. Other museums and galleries have many interesting pictures too, and it is good to make a habit of visiting them, looking for colors. You can also look in magazines, books, buildings, parks, and gardens.

Page 1

Paul Signac
Against the Enamel of a Background Rhythmic with Beats and Angles, Tones and Colors, Portrait of M Félix Fénéon 1890, 1890
Oil on canvas
29 1/8 x 38 x 5/8" (73.9 x 98.1 cm)
Private collection

The title conveys Signac's enthusiasm for real and imagined phenomena, expressed in pattern and little dots of color.

Page 2

Claude Monet
Water Lilies, c. 1920
Oil on canvas
One panel of a triptych, 6' 6" x 14'
(200 x 245 cm)
Mrs. Simon Guggenheim Fund

Interested in capturing fleeting aspects of light, Monet spent his last years painting his garden — here, the reflective lily pond, complete with sparkling water and hints of lilies, clouds, and sky.

Page 4

Edward Steichen
Moonrise, Mamaroneck, New York, 1904
Platinum, cyanotype, and ferroprussiate print
15 15/16 x 19" (38.9 x 48.3 cm)
Gift of the photographer
Reprinted with the permission of Joanna T. Steichen

Steichen carefully used his camera to frame a view of water and trees and awaited the perfect moment in the moonrise to make this still, moody photograph.

Page 5

Pablo Picasso
Two Acrobats with a Dog, 1905
Gouache on cardboard
41 1/2 x 29 1/2" (105.5 x 75 cm)
Gift of William A. M. Burden

While still quite young, Picasso frequently depicted offstage circus performers, emphasizing qualities of sadness and loneliness, perhaps thinking of their transient way of life.

Page 6

Willem de Kooning
Woman I, 1950-52
Oil on canvas
6' 3 7/8" x 58" (192.7 x 147.3 cm)
Purchase

Facial expression, aggressive lines, and angular shapes combine with harsh colors to create a kind of gigantic, frightful female in a series of paintings by de Kooning.

Page 7

Theo van Doesburg
(C. E. M. Küpper)
Simultaneous Counter-Composition, 1929-30
Oil on canvas
19 3/4 x 19 5/8" (50.1 x 49.8 cm)
The Sidney and Harriet Janis Collection

Geometry and color dominate in this work by van Doesburg. By tilting these blocks, he increased a sense of tension, as if tipping a careful, stable construction out of kilter.

Page 8

Vasily Kandinsky
Painting Number 201, 1914
Oil on canvas
64 1/4 x 48 1/4" (163 x 123.6 cm)
Nelson A. Rockefeller Fund
(by exchange)

Kandinsky was trying to capture
the sense of seasons and seasonal
change in a four-part series of which
this is one. He did not name the sea-
ons, but children may enjoy trying to
guess which one this might be.

Page 9

Josef Albers
Homage to the Square: Broad Call,
1967
Oil on composition board
48 x 48" (121.9 x 121.9 cm)
The Sidney and Harriet Janis
Collection

Albers's major interest was to
experiment with how colors interact
with each other optically. Look
particularly at the borders between
colors to see the subtle darkening
and lightening that occurs.

Page 10

Frank Stella
Abra Variation I, 1969
Fluorescent alkyd paint on canvas
10' x 9' 11 7/8" (305 x 304.5 cm)
Gift of Philip Johnson in honor of
William Rubin

Stella composed pictures using
geometric motifs and also explored
the optical properties of color. Here
he confined himself to the square
and semicircle, allowing you to find a
logic by following the arcs as they
weave through others.

Page 11

Frank Stella
Kastūra, 1979
Oil and epoxy on aluminum, wire
mesh. 9' 7" x 7' 8" x 30"
(292 x 233.5 x 76.1 cm) (irregular)
Acquired through the Mr. and Mrs.
Victor Ganz, Mr. and Mrs. Donald H.
Peters, and Mr. and Mrs. Charles
Zadok Funds

Here Stella used many shapes, cut
out and assembled in a jumble of
contrasting colors. Try comparing
the two Stella compositions to see
the ways in which they are alike and
different.

Page 12

Irving Penn
Still Life with Watermelon, 1947
Dye-transfer print
24 x 19 7/8" (60.9 x 50.5 cm)
Gift of the photographer

Penn chose to make this image
in color, photographing fruit with
intense hues against a stark
background to emphasize a lush
overripeness.

Page 13

Ernst Ludwig Kirchner
Street, Dresden, 1908
(dated on painting 1907)
Oil on canvas
59 1/4" x 6' 6 7/8" (150.5 x 200.4 cm)
Purchase

Called an Expressionist, Kirchner
selected colors to elicit emotional
responses, in this case perhaps
making a judgment on the German
bourgeoisie.

Page 14

Vasily Kandinsky
Murnau Landscape, 1909
Oil on paper
27 1/4 x 37" (69.2 x 93.9 cm)
Promised gift of an anonymous
donor

Colors of nature are intensified in
this thickly brushed painting of a
village and mountain meadow by
Kandinsky, who later painted color-
filled abstractions, such as the one
on page 8.

Page 15

Odilon Redon
Vase of Flowers, 1914
Pastel on paper
28 3/4 x 21 1/8" (73 x 53.7 cm)
Gift of William S. Paley

Redon sought timeless beauty in a
vase of cut flowers, evincing the
mysterious, gentle power of nature.